A Miscellany of Haiku

by Seren Langley and David Breslin

Print-on-demand UK edition

Softback: ISBN 978-1-917974-00-4
Kindle: ISBN 978-1-917974-10-3
eBook: ISBN 978-1-917974-12-7
Audiobook: ISBN 978-1-917974-11-0

Author site https://vitareginae.wordpress.com or follow on social media @sherdnerdess.

Like this title?
Please leave us a review on your chosen site.

Contents

For my wonderful mumsie, Marian 1951–2022.

Introduction

A selection of 14 Japanese-style short poems in *Haiku*, *Senryū* and *Tanka* formats in British English with some translations into authentic script and Romanised phonetics. The Japanese text is in traditional alignment, so read right-to-left and top-to-bottom. Where poems are bilingual, the syllable count works in both. They are observations about amusements in the mundane world, with notes to give more background to the narrative. I have cheated with the meter in places by cropping long vowels and merging the syllabic *n* sound. This compilation will be available in print and included as part of a forth-coming short story collection, provisionally titled *View From the Window*, with audiobook version.

Haiku [俳句] is a developed literary art form from Japan using 17 syllables only across 3 lines in the format 5-7-5. The style was originally part of a court entertainment called *Renga* [連歌] where a pair or group would collaborate to create several verses in syllable pattern 5-7-5 7-7 (called *Tanka* [短歌] as a standalone, of which I have written some examples). *Haiku* are meant to express ordinary life and celebrate nature with lyricism. Usually, they contain a technical cutting word [*kireji* - 切れ字] at the end of one line to change the focus, and seasonal hints too [*kigo* - 季語]. They are not meant to have titles nor punctuation but humour is permitted under the rules of less formal *Senryū* [川柳], and rhyming is optional.

1

Earth's inconstant friend
silver in the endless sky
life keeps on turning

2

a single orb hangs
lonely in the open sky
watching over all

in a hate-divided world
reminding us we are one

3

like a shaggy dog
verdant cedars scatter their
flakes of captured snow

4

like a shaggy dog
swaying cedars scatter their
spheres of settled rain

5

there is nothing so
soothing as a purring cat
content on one's lap

6

my Schrödinger's flat;
will the admin never end?
keys in hand - alive!

7

the wasp has much gall
for oak to grow her children
and not new acorns

8

the Olympic Games
dreams, victories and defeats
tears fall like blossoms

オリンピック
夢勝ち負かし
涙散る

Orimpikku
yume kachi makashi
namida chiru

Version previously published in *Blithe Spirit* Volume
34.3, p79 (August 2024), quarterly Journal of the
British Haiku Society.org.uk, ed. Iliyana STOYANOVA
with thanks.

9

bin truck 6AM
vehicle is reversing
insomnia reigns

不　車　夜
眠　後　明
位　進　け
い　　　塵ゴﾐ

yoake gomi
kuruma koushin
fumin kurai

10

security lights
fireflies glow in darkness
insomnia reigns

安全灯
蛍闇照る
不眠位い

anzen hi
hotaru yami teru
fumin kurai

11

wild dolphins hunt
in busy Atlantic seas
where awed humans gawp

海豚には
込み海で狩る
人間アングリ

イルカ

iruka niwa
komi umi de karu
ningen anguri

12

Common dolphins scout
in crowded ocean waters
where awed humans sail

真海豚に
込み海で斥候
人間帆走

Ma-iruka ni
komi umi de sekkou
ningen hansou

13

Mother is full-up
she has eaten too much
pizza and ice cream

sprawling like a starfish in
Mediterranean heat

母が一杯
ピザやジェラートを
食べ過ぎた

Haha ga ippai
pizza ya jerāto (w)o
tabesugita

14

Seren is full-up
with parents she has eaten
far too much tapas

星が一杯
親とタパスを
食べ過ぎた

Hoshi ga ippai
Oya to* tapasu (w)o
tabesugita

* The particle to [と] means 'with' rather than 'and'
here. It has two functions in Japanese grammar.

Contributions from David Breslin

Taken from Twitter/𝕏

Used with full permission and knowledge of the author @Breslinzilla [https://x.com/Breslinzilla] after a brief phase on that platform in July 2013. He took the opportunity of this publication to bring these 8 verses to a different audience. David is a published classical musician and independent singer-songwriter based in York, UK [www.uymp.co.uk/composers/david-breslin/] Listen to his compositions on the popular distribution site BandCamp [https://davidbreslin.bandcamp.com/] and see his current projects via *Voicemail from Neptune* on Wordpress [https://davidbreslin.wordpress.com/].

soberly learning
Twitter-use for work so a
queuing-test haiku

a whole one-hundred
and forty characters? I
don't need that many!

at one with nature
cool! check out my new ringtone!
wood-pigeons scatter

from a safe distance
the sound of cars on wet roads
is oddly soothing

concrete-sided stream
bears empty cans and bottles
water lilies too

from dawn-stroked tarmac
the young starling rises
helped by a kestrel

relax - food - TV -
X-Files: killer cockroaches!
couscous everywhere

unplug my guitar
press headstock to tabletop
notes sound like distance

Index of First Lines

Notes

1 Author David Lanoue mentions the act of moon-gazing at various points in his 2000 work *Haiku Guy* [ASIN B008JERD5O]. This is an important consideration for the style, so here is my take for posterity. The moon has always been one of my favourite celestial objects anyway. It was never man-in-the-moon when I was growing up - we only had Lady Moon, in the ancient Celtic tradition. I had many problems finalising this piece because every attempt sounded too derivative. Eventually, I worked out why. I had been channelling a poem that I learned as a child, *Silver* [https://allpoetry.com/poem/8494557-Silver-by-Walter-de-la-Mare] by Walter de la Mare (1913 in *Peacock Pie*, ASIN B0082QU8XI in US). There is an alternative version using 'eternal' in the first line instead of 'inconstant', which changes the tone.

2 Another riff on moon-gazing but could also be read as the Sun. This one is more topical to the ongoing wars is Syria, Yemen and Ukraine. The refugees they have created are seemingly unwelcome everywhere. In a call for international compassion and tolerance, the *Tanka* composition became more political than I was aiming for but I was too pleased with the finished verse to omit it.

3–4 I was watching out the glass door at the back garden of the in-laws' house while unwell over a Christmas break. A sudden gust caused the larger, lower branches of the mature trees to shed their load onto the grass. The action reminded me of a dog drying itself after mischief in a river or puddle. Multiple presentation is in keeping with the traditional style from printed art where designers would introduce an alternative profile or colour palette. If the alliteration is too much, replace 'spheres' with 'drops' or the final line of either version with 'precipitation'.

5 In honour of friends' aged cats, Pebbles the tuxedo in Hadham, Hertfordshire and Kitty the tortoiseshell of Cookham, Berkshire. Both were picky about who they graced with affection and I saw them in the same week, with cuddles. I felt very privileged! Alternatively, use 'on one's cosy lap' for the last line.

6 It is a pun on a famous thought experiment by Dr Erwin Schrödinger (1887–1961) to help explain quantum theory. Stay with me. A hypothetical cat is in a box with a radioactive substance which randomly decays, causing fatality. Until the box is opened, it is impossible to know for certain whether the imaginary cat is alive or dead. I refused to believe the newly-purchased property could really be mine until I actually collected the keys. It was a big day. The flat is amazing with a view over the river and low flood risk.

7 Yes, I know, this pun is terrible too. I am disproportionately proud of it. The verse was inspired by a fascinating segment in a Sir David Attenborough episode of *Life in the Undergrowth*. The clip is available on YouTube [https://youtu.be/CzXccvoJThI] from 2008 © BBC Studios and redone for *Wild Isles*: Episode 2 - Woodland (2023) [https://www.bbc.co.uk/programmes/p0f21jy9]. I saw galls in action walking on the footpaths near my parents' house while sorting it for probate sale.

8 Written first in Japanese for the closing ceremony of the 2020 32nd Olympiad held in Tokyo, Japan over the following summer due to global issues with the pandemic. I agonised over the last verb, whether to use the strict word, *or chiru* (for flowers) or *furu* [降る] (for raindrops) as 'fall'. I settled on the flowers version because I want the ambiguity of it being a happy or sad occasion. With success or failure, "heartache or elation" as one commentator said, the next competition may bring the opposite result. It is for the reader to decide the tone, otherwise it would be too dreary.

The verb used is a conscious, considered and deliberate choice. It is supposed to suggest the cultural connotations of transience, at the fore during cherry blossom [*sakura -* 桜] season, and associates it to the famous Iroha verse. There are several options for the non-literary verb: *na.ku* [泣] (people) OR [鳴] (animals) to mean 'cry', or *afu.ru* [溢] to mean 'overflow'. None other fitted what I wanted. As with English, grammar is more lax in poetry than in everyday life.

I wrote a second version which changes the verb conjugation at the end of the middle line to become: ... 負けは // なみだ散る. Rather than *wa* being a particle here, read the Kana phonetically as **ha** to create the phrase *hana-mi da chiru* [花見だ散る] - watching blossoms fall. The changed script is a clue to make it more obvious what I intend without changing the shared English translation. However, it feels too overworked for the medium so is excluded from having its own entry.

9–10 A couplet. Most of us have been there. Unable sleep for no apparent reason and the random things that disturb precious slumbers. One is a green courtesy light directly outside my partner's bedroom window which stays on all night, the other is the waste collection lorry arriving far too early in the morning for comfort. I have put the safety announcement in monospaced text to indicate its simulated voice and for added humour value.

11–12 It was me. I was the gawping human. I saw dolphins in the wild with my mum off the Portuguese coast from Tavira, Algarve. It was one of the last times we were able to be together before her illness developed. We had been trying to do the trip for years, but kept having to be at the quayside in other cities too early for bus connections. There was finally a tour the week we were there and in the correct place. It was worth the wait. They were so gorgeous and playful. A source of much excitement. A dream come true. Of course, the word 'dolphins' has to be said in the way of squeeing at a pitch so high only dogs or themselves can hear. It warranted two similar compositions. *Anguri* is an obscure piece of vocabulary meaning 'open-mouthed', that I got from a dictionary to fit the meter (<u>not</u> a transliteration of *angry*). 'Common' is the species name of the *Delphinus delphis* we saw, not a frequency qualifier so is written with a capital letter. The lines can be a mix-and-match arrangement when kept in order. See more about this event in my forthcoming European and Animal travelogues.

13–14 These are also comedic and I have not put the pair forward for external publication. We were in Palermo, the capital of the island of Sicily, Italy. My mum was being silly while we were hot and stuffed on lunch. She demanded I write her a *Haiku*-style poem to commemorate the situation during our holiday. I obliged and this was the carefully(!) crafted result a short time later. It made her laugh so much and is a very precious memory now she is gone. The original English-only extension was '*laying* like a starfish', but it did not convey quite the right image and is not translated. I adapted it later for another anecdote when the in-laws came to visit taking inspiration from a meal at York Fossgate branch of Ambiente restaurant [https://www.ambiente-tapas.co.uk/fossgate]. The given names *Seren* and *Hoshi* both mean 'star' in their respective languages so it is a direct translation from Welsh to Japanese.

Further Interest

BOUTWELL, Clay and Yumi (eds) var *Learn Japanese through Haiku: Enjoy Japanese culture while building your vocabulary and grammar*, TheJapanShop.com, Bundle B0DGJF7T89:
- 2021 MATSUO Bashō, ASIN B09G74F297;
- 2024 MASAOKA Shiki, ASIN B0DGJ9JVZ7;
- 2024 KOBAYASHI Issa, ASIN B0DJDL787S;
- 2025 YOSA Buson, ASIN B0F7MZDT5B.

BOWERS, Faubion (ed) 2012 *The Classic Tradition of Haiku*: An Anthology, Dover Thrift Editions, ASIN B00B7VWLTY.

COBB, David (ed) 2002 *The British Museum: Haiku*, The British Museum Press, ISBN 978-0714124018 (print only).

COLE, Chris J. 2017 *The Silence Between Moments: A collection of moments captured in haiku, tanka, cherita and prose poetry*, Poetry in Motion Authoring, ASIN B072J4RCDH.

DONEGAN, Patricia 2010 *haiku mind: 108 Poems to Cultivate Awareness & Open Your Heart*, Shambhala Reprint, ASIN B00ATMWJV2.

DONEGAN, Patricia & ISHIBASHI Yoshie 2025 *The Poetry of Chiyo-ni: The Life and Art of Japan's Most Celebrated Woman Haiku Master*, Tuttle Publishing (forthcoming).

HIRSHFIELD, Jane 2011 *The Heart of Haiku*, Amazon Singles, ASIN B0057IYMF4.

HU, Jennifer 2013 *Collected Haiku: 280 verses inspired by Zen practice*, ASIN B00D9HS8P0 (and her 2014 releases).

KERN, Adam L. 2018 *The Penguin Book of Haiku*, Penguin Classics, ASIN B073W4FMFQ.

KOBAYASHI Issa &
- Sam HAMILL (trans) 1997 *The Spring of My Life and Selected Haiku*, ASIN B00DUGS7CY.
- David LANOUE (trans) 2019 *A Taste of Issa*, ASIN B07VG66W83.

LANOUE, David 2020 *Haiku Guy Omnibus: A 20th Anniversary Edition of Haiku Guy, Laughing Buddha, Haiku Wars, Frog Poet, and Dewdrop World*, HaikuGuy.com, ASIN B085DM1BXL.

MABIN, Alta H. 2021 *Learn the art of Haiku & Tanka*, Print Replica Editions, ASIN B09B5H58MF.

MAGUIRE, Phill 2016 *Haiku, Senryu & Tanka*, independent publishing, ASIN B01M30DV03 (unavailable).

MATSUO Bashō & Lucien STRYK (trans) 1985 *On Love and Barley*, Penguin Classics, ASIN B002RI9BG2.

PILBEAM, Mavis (ed) 2010 *The British Museum: Haiku Animals*, The British Museum Press, ISBN 978-0714124612 (print only).

SHARMA, Shashidhar 2021 *How to Write Haiku - A Beginner's Guide*, Monk Key Series, ASIN B093DWRH44.

various with Michael HALDANE (trans) 2022 *Bashō and the Haikuists* (incl YOSA Buson, MASAOKA Shiki, FUKUDA Chiyo-ni etc), Delphi Collected Works, ASIN B09RGB2M6R.

WILSON, William Scott 2023 *A Beginner's Guide to Japanese Haiku: Major Works by Japan's Best-Loved Poets - From Basho and Issa to Ryokan and Santoka, with Works by Six Women Poets*, Tuttle Publishing, ASIN B0BMB3VC6Z.

YAMAMOTO, Mai 2019 *Haiku & Tanka Practice: Insights of a Japanese poet*, independent publishing, ASIN B07YS9BFFH.

About the Author

Seren is an archaeologist by training but converted to computing due to an early career injury. She now works in medical research, building databases. Her school was a designated language college in Hertfordshire, so she was able to learn Japanese formally there and has carried on with these studies ever since to create these vaguely coherent self-translated bilingual verses. Seren achieved a long-held dream to visit Japan touring Honshū in 2014 with her mother. She has settled in York, UK with her partner and far too many books!

She is formerly the Information Assistant for the Council for British Archaeology [https://www.archaeologyuk.org/] (CBA) and edited the Briefing events section of their *British Archaeology* magazine for many years. Outside of work, Seren enjoys reading and cataloguing her vast array of books, blogging reviews, studying various online courses, genealogical research, plus film and theatre trips. By self-admission, she has no manual artistic skills so relies on words and data for all her creative pursuits. This is her first self-publication.

Author site vitareginae.wordpress.com or follow on social media @sherdnerdess.

Acknowledgements

My thanks to various sounding boards - partner Andy Sherman, his dad Keith, Louisa Knight, Clare Sangster, colleagues at the University of Leeds for all the encouragement and regulars of Bookcrossing Meetup in York for being my test group. **Like this title?** Please leave us a review on your chosen site. Look out for the follow-up collection of poetry, and other titles too. Thank you for reading.

www.ingramcontent.com/pod-product-compliance
Lightning Source LLC
Chambersburg PA
CBHW071801020426
42331CB00008B/2355